WING CHUN
BIL JEE

The Deadly Art
of Thrusting Fingers
BY WILLIAM CHEUNG

DISCLAIMER

Please note that the publisher of this instructional book is NOT RESPONSIBLE in any manner whatsoever for any injury which may occur by reading and/or following the instructions herein.

It is essential that before following any of the activities, physical or otherwise, herein described, the reader or readers should first consult his or her physician for advice on whether or not the reader or readers should embark on the physical activity described herein. Since the physical activities described herein may be too sophisticated in nature, it is *essential that a physician be consulted.*

©**UNIQUE PUBLICATIONS INC., 1983**

All rights reserved
Printed in the United States of America
ISBN: 0-86568-045-0
Library of Congress No.: 83-050021

 **UNIQUE PUBLICATIONS**

4201 VANOWEN PLACE, BURBANK, CA 91505

Table of Contents

Profile of William Cheung

Master William Cheung has over thirty years experience in Wing Chun and stands eighth in the direct line of grandmasters from its originator, Ng Mui. At the age of ten, in 1951, he began taking instruction from Grandmaster Yip Man. At fourteen, he chose Wing Chun as a way of life, and studied full-time under the roof of his master for another four years.

In Hong Kong, 1957, William Cheung won the kung fu elimination contest against opponents with years more experience than himself and helped teach the late Bruce Lee many of the techniques used later by Lee in his successful film career.

To pursue an academic career in Australia, Master Cheung left Hong Kong in 1959. Along with academics, he continued to study and practice Wing Chun and held various positions in the Sydney judo clubs, including the 1770 Club and the Blacktown Club. As they were the only martial arts clubs in existence at the time, they provided the only way to promote the teaching of Wing Chun. In 1965, Master Cheung started the first Wing Chun kung fu club at the Australian National University at Canberra. Then after finishing his university studies in 1969, he devoted himself to theoretical research studies of Wing Chun and giving private lessons to a group of dedicated students. Many of these students now have their own schools.

The year 1974 was also busy for William Cheung; he founded his Australian Wing Chun Academy in Melbourne and saw to the founding of the Australian Kung Fu Federation. of which he is chairman. He was then nominated to represent the Federation at a meeting with the Australian Department of Youth, Sport, and Recreation for the purpose of creating an Australian Martial Arts Council.

More recently, Master Cheung has starred in his first movie, a Golden Harvest Film Company production of *Wing Chun Kung Fu.* He has been appointed chief instructor for unarmed combat at the U.S. Navy base in Yokosuka, Japan, and has lectured at Dan Inosanto's Martial Arts Academy, California Martial Arts Academy, and the Degerberg Martial Arts Academy in Chicago. He has also penned *The Mystery of Bruce Lee* and appeared in cover stories for numerous international magazines.

Deeply disturbed by the adverse publicity of kung fu, and by the misbeliefs and doubts expressed by many people, Cheung has devoted his life to preserving the authentic teachings of Wing Chun. He strongly believes that by giving people confidence in their own ability to protect themselves against physical attack, they'll no longer fear attack. And when fear is removed, the arrogance of uncertainty will be dispelled; thus the need to *prove* oneself in any form of physical combat will no longer be necessary. His teaching, therefore, is concerned with the suppression of violent action, not its promotion. This is taught at all his schools worldwide—in New Zealand, Hong Kong, the U.S., Australia, Germany, and Japan.

Forward

It is a privilege to write an introduction for *Wing Chun Bil Jee, The Deadly Art of Thrusting Fingers* by Master William Cheung (Cheung Chuk Hing), who is considered the number one fighter in the Wing Chun clan by the majority of its practitioners.

My training in Wing Chun began in 1964 under the late Bruce Lee. During this training, Lee often told many stories about Cheung's prowess as a street fighter in Hong Kong. When he spoke of Bill Cheung, he spoke with respect. It was Bill Cheung, his senior in the Wing Chun system who helped train him to win the Hong Kong championships in 1957, and from whom he learned some of the concepts that later led to the creation of his Jeet Kune Do.

After witnessing Master Cheung demonstrate and perform Wing Chun, I stand in awe of his style. He is the number one authority in the original Wing Chun system, which contains superior footwork and entry techniques that the modified version lacks.

I consider *Wing Chun Bil Jee, The Deadly Art of Thrusting Fingers* a great contribution, not only to the Wing Chun style and its practitioners, but to the martial arts world in general.

Dan Inosanto

Dan Inosanto

From the title of this book it would be natural to assume that Master Cheung regards the fingers as potentially the most important weapon in fighting. Do not be misled. He believes ultimately in the power of the human brain—intelligence, the ability to reason logically and to systematize and analyze—will overcome the random use of force.

A supremely analytical martial artist, Master Cheung is world famous for his ability to practice what he preaches. Yet, many cannot see beyond the speed and power of his movements to the mind and intelligence directing them. To train in Wing Chun under Master William Cheung is to be initiated into a world in which ironclad rules of logic reign supreme. He teaches a complete, scientific system of fighting and continually stresses that the student must not merely do, he must understand.

The Wing Chun system is a uniquely scientific fighting style. The thrusting fingers are an integral part of it and Master Cheung does more than merely explain the mechanics of the Bil Jee form itself; he offers the thinking martial artist insight into the conceptual framework from which most of its efficacy is derived.

Much has been said over the years of the author's achievements in the martial arts sphere, but little has been said of the man, William Cheung. During the short time I've known him, his multifaceted personality has made a considerable impact on me. Although he's a serious thinker and philosopher, his sense of humor is ever-present and infectious; a charismatic figure, he is not easily impressed and displays a light-hearted irreverence towards stuffiness and authority; always an optimist, he is full of plans and ideas; a widely knowledgeable and educated man, he enjoys many activities outside of kung fu and lives life to the fullest. To those who know him, he exhibits a warmth and generosity of spirit rarely encountered and believes wholeheartedly in the qualities of integrity, trust and faithfulness that form the basis of real friendship.

As a teacher, Master William Cheung exemplifies the spirit of kung fu and is therefore greatly loved and respected by his students.

Guy West

Preface

Few people realize the potential of fingers for use as a weapon. Most lack the knowledge of their proper usage. Even to other Wing Chun masters, Bil Jee is a mystery. It's the most advanced form of kung fu.

Originally, Grandmaster Yip Man regarded the entire Wing Chun system as a secret and felt it should not be passed on to anybody. He taught, instead, modified versions of Wing Chun movements and techniques. Because of these modifications, explanations behind Bil Jee movements are vague and inadequate, the efficiency of the techniques are drastically reduced, and the essence is completely lost.

Twenty-eight years ago, I was chosen by my late Grandmaster Yip Man to solely inherit the original art of Wing Chun. But before I was taught the authentic version, I took an oath not to reveal the secret to anyone during his lifetime. The oath included the suppression of the true Bil Jee form.

Grandmaster Yip Man passed away in 1972.

As an art, Wing Chun can only survive the test of time if it is maintained in a healthy state. When thousands of pracititioners are doing Wing Chun the wrong way, it affects the good name of the art. For this reason alone, the secret must be revealed.

Wing Chun Bil Jee, The Deadly Art of Thrusting Fingers is my first undertaking to accomplish this task.

William Cheung

Cheung Chuk Hing

Acknowledgements

Many people have directly and indirectly helped with this book. In particular I would like to thank Mr. Curtis Wong, President of Unique Publications, for publishing this book, Stuart Goldman, editor, for his encouragement and patience; Mark Komuro for the lay-out and design; Eddie Ikuta, the best photographer in and out of the martial arts, for his keen eye and expert timing; Margaret Tajiri for sales promotion; Harry Wong for his assistance and courage in posing opposite the deadly thrusting fingers; Dan Inosanto, one of the most accomplished martial artists in the world, for his time and friendship, and finally, Guy West, my student and friend, for making the teaching of Wing Chun a rewarding profession.

A Letter from Bruce Lee
January 6, 1969

William,

I was looking over my old mail and found most of the letters you wrote me. The latest one, or the latest one that I found, has this address. So I write this letter in hope that even if you have moved, somehow or another, this will reach you.

It has been nearly ten year now since I've been in the States and when I sit down some evening, lost in my recollection of my memories, you are among one of those that often pop up. I sincerely hope you and your family are enjoying the best of everything.

During the last ten year, Chinese martial art has always been a major part of my activity, though I am now in a new field, the field of acting. My achievement in the martial art is most satisfying and the word 'Chinese' has come a long way in the circle of martial art due to the fact that all three of the U.S. Karate free-style champs are studying under me. William, I've lost faith in the Chinese classical art — though I still call mine Chinese — because basically all styles are product of land swimming, even the 詠春 school. So my line of training is more toward efficient street fighting with everything goes, wearing head gear, gloves, chest guard, shin knee guards, etc. For the past five year now I've been training the hardest and for a purpose, not just dissipated hit-miss training. I'm running every day, sometime up to six miles. I've named my style jeet kune do 截拳道 —— reason for my not sticking to 詠春 because I sincerely feel that this style has more to offer regarding efficiency. I mentioned all the above because it is a major event in my life and like to fill you in with it.

I've been doing good too in the field of acting. I don't know whether or not you've seen my TV series the 'Green Hornet' in Australia, but

I've just bought a half acre home in
Bel-Air on top of a hill — plenty of fresh
air — like living out in the country, but tough
on the calf running around the hill side.

Well my friend, all in all, that's what
has happened to me —— I don't know whether
this will reach you I hope it will.

Anyway, my warmest regard to your family
and do drop me a line I would like to
hear from you
                                    Your friend
                                    Bruce Lee

I've worked for a year in it, setting up a good foundation.
Occasionally I appear on T.V. and Movie. The latest
one is an MGM production "Little Sister" with James
Gardner that should be coming out in a few
months. I'm in the process of forming a production
company with a few important backers here in
the States, concentrating on producing martial
art movies, T.V. series, etc.

Chapter 1

Wing Chun History

Origins of Wing Chun

The origin of Wing Chun can be found in the turbulent, repressive Ching Dynasty of over 250 years ago. It was a time when 90 percent of the Chinese, the Hans, were ruled by the ten percent minority, the Manchus.

When all weapons were outlawed by the Manchus, the Hans began training a revolutionary army in the art of kung fu. The Sil Lum temple became the secret sanctuary for preparatory trainings of a classical style which took between 15 to 20 years for each person to master.

To develop a new form, one which would have a shorter training time, five of China's grandmasters met to discuss the merits of each of the various forms of kung fu. By choosing the most efficient techniques from each style, they developed training programs that would develop an efficient martial artist in five to seven years, one third the original time. However, before this new form could be put into practice, the Sil Lum temple was raided and burned by the Manchus.

Ng Mui, a nun, was the only survivor of the original five grandmasters. She passed her knowledge onto a young orphan girl, who she'd named Wing Chun. The name represented "hope for the future." In turn, Wing Chun shared her knowledge with her husband, Leung Bok Cho.

Through the years, the style became known as Wing Chun. Its techniques and teaching were passed onto a few, always carefully selected students.

Nearly 100 years ago, Leung Jun was one of the chosen students to receive training in Wing Chun. He lived with his two sons, Leung Bak and Leung Cheun in a prosperous Chinese city, Fatshan. Aside from his fame as a martial artist, Leung Jun owned an herbal shop. He was greatly respected by his community as a gentleman and a scholar, one who never boasted of his kung fu ability.

Chan Wah Soon was a money changer with a shop next door to Leung Jun's. He was a large, strong man, who admired his neighbor's Wing Chun ability. When Leung Jun chose to keep his art within his family and not take any outside students, Chan Wah Soon resorted to spying on Leung Jun's daily teachings to his sons. Leung Jun soon learned of Chan's spying and deliberately taught a modified version when Chan was watching.

Chan's dedication to spying eventually touched Leung Jun and he was eventually accepted as a disciple. However, Leung Jun continued to teach only the modified version to Chan because he feared that after his own death, Chan would dispute the Wing Chun grandmastership with his sons. Since Chan was a much larger and stronger man, neither of Leung Jun's sons could have defeated him if Chan had learned the real version of Wing Chun.

Leung Jun's suspicions of Chan Wah Soon were well founded in reality. When Leung Jun and his son Leung Cheun died, Chan drove the surviving son, Leung Bak, from Fatshan.

Leung Bak settled in Hong Kong.

Chan Wah Soon wasted little time in teaching the modified version of Wing Chun to selected disciples. He enjoyed tremendous popularity, but after many years had accepted only eleven students.

Then a twelve-year-old boy, Yip Man, came to Chan Wah Soon with 300 pieces of silver asking for acceptance as his final disciple. At first, Chan assumed the boy stole the money from his parents. He accompanied Yip Man home, confronted his parents, and discovered that Yip Man had indeed saved the silver by himself. Admiring Yip Man's dedication, Chan accepted him as his last disciple.

Yip Man studied Chan's Wing Chun system for four years and after Chan's death, moved to Hong Kong. By the age of sixteen, he had the reputation of an accomplished martial artist. Through some of his martial arts friends, Yip Man was introduced to an eccentric old man with renowned kung fu ability. Yip Man challenged the old eccentric and lost dismally. The old man was Leung Bak, Lueng Jun's surviving son of the original Wing Chun system. After the encounter, Leung Bak told Yip Man the story of the modified version and accepted him as his only student.

Yip Man studied the authentic version of Wing Chun for four years. With his new knowledge, he returned to Fatshan, defeated his seniors in the modifed system and became the grandmaster of Wing Chun. All kung fu practitioners of China respected him for his kung fu ability, but he never accepted any disciples.

In 1948, when the Communists took over China, Yip Man left for Macao, leaving his fortune behind. In Macao, Leung Shan, a master of White Eyebrow kung fu, found Yip Man in an impoverished state and took him to Hong Kong, where he cared for him.

Leung Shan had a kung fu school on the premises of the Restaurant Worker's Union in Hong Kong. Yip Man was given a small apartment there. Every night, after the restaurant closed, kung fu classes were conducted at the Worker's Union. Often, Yip Man watched the classes in progress, and without malice, ridiculed the inadequacy of Leung Shan's style.

One night in 1951, Leung Shan became angered by Yip Man's disrespect. To teach Yip Man a lesson, he challenged him. Though Leung Shan was larger and younger than Yip Man, he was no match for the art of Wing Chun and was easily defeated.

After defeating Leung Chan, Yip Man revealed himself as the grandmaster of Wing Chun and took Leung Shan as his first disciple of a few, always carefully selected students.

Yip Man

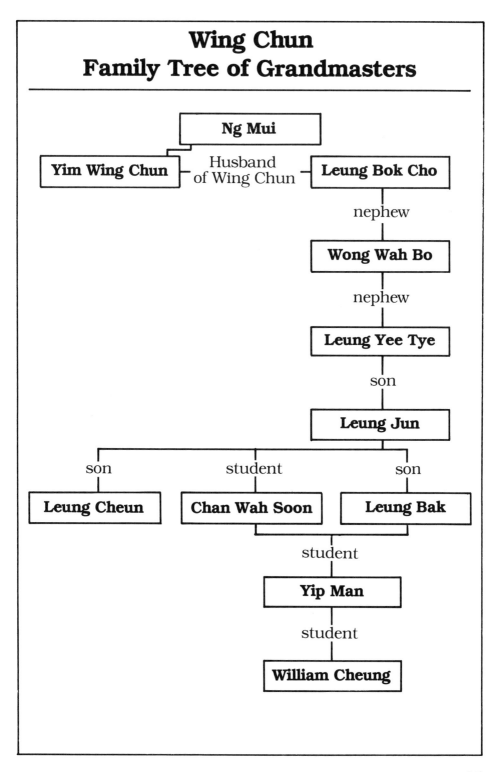

Wing Chun
Family Tree of Grandmasters

Ng Mui

Yim Wing Chun — Husband of Wing Chun — Leung Bok Cho

nephew

Wong Wah Bo

nephew

Leung Yee Tye

son

Leung Jun

son — Leung Cheun

student — Chan Wah Soon

son — Leung Bak

student

Yip Man

student

William Cheung

Chapter 2

Basic Arm Movements of Wing Chun

The Wing Chun guard position is included with each arm movement as a reference point from which to begin.

Tan Sao, Palm-up Arm

1) Wing Chun guard

2) Tan sao

Side View of Tan Sao

1)

2)

Bon Sao, Wing Arm

1) Wing Chun guard

2) Bon sao

Side View of Bon Sao

1)

2)

Fok Sao, Bridge-on Arm

Side View of Fok Sao

1) Wing Chun guard

1)

2) Fok sao

2)

Kan Sao, Splitting Block

1) Wing Chun guard

2) Intermediate move to kan sao.

3) Kan sao

Side View of Kan Sao

1)

2)

3)

Jut Sao, Jerk Arm

1) Wing Chun guard

2) Jut sao

Side View of Jut Sao

1)

2)

Cheun Sao, Threading Arm

Side View of Cheun Sao

1) Wing Chun guard

1)

2) Intermediate move to cheun sao.

2)

3) Cheun sao

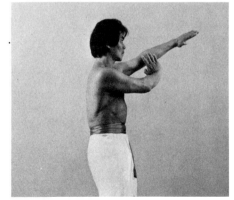

3)

Gum Sao, Pinning Arm

1) Wing Chun guard

2) Intermediate move to gum sao.

3) Gum sao

Side View of Gum Sao

1)

2)

3)

Fut Sao, Swinging Arm

Side View of Fut Sao

1) Wing Chun guard

1)

2) Intermediate move to fut sao.

2)

3) Fut sao

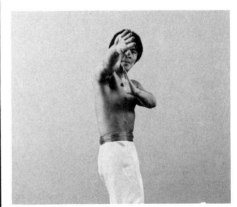

3)

Pak Sao, Slapping Block	**Side View of Pak Sao**

1) Wing Chun guard

1)

2) Pak sao

2)

Side Tarn Sao, Bounce-off Arm   Side View of Tarn Sao

1) Wing Chun guard

1)

2) Intermediate move to side tarn sao.

2)

3) Side tarn sao.

3)

27

Underneath Tarn Sao, Bounce-off Arm

1) Wing Chun guard

2) Underneath tarn sao.

Side View of Underneath Tarn Sao

1)

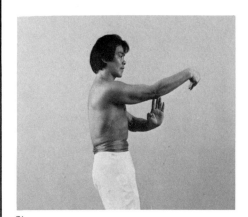

2)

Quan Sao, a Tan Sao and Bon Sao Deflection Block

Side View of Quan Sao

1) Wing Chun guard

1)

2) Intermediate move to quan sao.

2)

3) Quan sao

3)

29

Larp Sao

1) Wing Chun guard.

2) Slightly lowering right arm, turn it inward and . . .

3) bring forearm in towards chest and . . .

4) upward and . . .

5) outward and . . .

6) extended.

Side View of Larp Sao

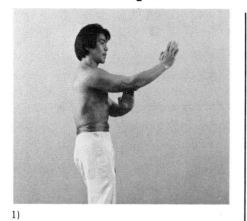

1)

4)

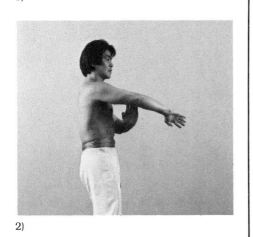

2)

5)

3)

6)

Huen Sao, Rotation Hand

1) Lead arm extended with palm up.

4) outward and upward.

2) Bring hand straight back and rotate it inward and . . .

5) Turn palm inward vertically and cock it back at wrist.

3) downward and . . .

Side View of Huen Sao

1)

4)

2)

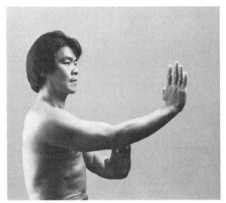

5)

3)

Po Pi Tserng, Double Palm Strike

1) Wing Chun guard.

3) Step forward with left leg and . . .

2) Bring right wrist to left wrist.

4) double palm strike.

Side View of Po Pi Tserng

1)

3)

2)

4)

Bil Sao, Thrusting Arm

1) Wing Chun guard

2) Bil sao

Side View of Bil Sao

1)

2)

Chapter 3

Wing Chun Training System

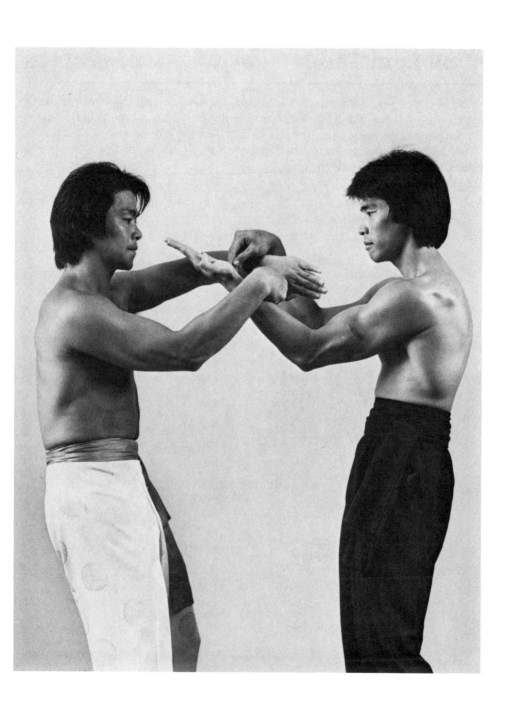

A. Sil Lum Tao

The *Sil Lum Tao* form trains breathing, concentration, coordination, arm movement, mind and body coordination, independent movement of the limbs in relation to the body, and balance of the neutral stance.

The *neutral stance* is the most efficient stance. It allows for a practitioner to move freely in any direction.

Neutral stance. Stand with feet parallel to each other and slightly wider than shoulder width. Body weight is evenly distributed on both feet. Legs are bent so that the center is lowered to middle body height.

Side view of neutral stance.

B. Chum Kil

Chum Kil means "bridging the gap or finding the opponent's bridge."

This form practices the different front, side, and backward steps that avoid direct confrontation with an opponent's force. It carries on the essentials of the Sil Lum Tao form, but expands the training of mobility, coordination of arms and legs, and the combinations of kicks.

The following photos are examples of movements practiced in Chum Kil.

Side Step Right Bon Sao

1) Wing Chun guard.　　　　　　　　　　2) Side step with right leg and right bon sao.

Bil Sao and Front Kick

1) Wing Chun guard

3) Front kick

2) Side step and bil sao

4) Step forward with Wing Chun guard

Side View of Bil Sao and Front Kick

1)

3)

2)

4)

C. Chi Sao

Chi Sao is an exercise for improving close distance focusing with the eyes and *contact reflexes.*

After a block, there exists a *contact point.* At this point, an opponent's intended move is transmitted as a vibration. The response to this vibration is a contact reflex action.

The principle behind contact reflexes is similar to that of fishing. When a fishing line is in the water, the fisherman doesn't have to see the bait taken to know there's a fish on the line. When a fish strikes the bait, there's a vibration on the line and the fisherman feels the movement where he holds the rod—the contact point.

In Wing Chun training for developing contact reflexes, the practitioner attempts to interrupt an opponent's next movement from the vibration at the point of contact and counter instantly.

The side benefits of chi sao exercises are improvements in mobility at close range, timing of movements, accuracy of strike, generation of power at short range, and control of an opponent's balance and arms from point of contact.

There are three stages of chi sao training:
a) single handed chi sao, parallel armed
b) single handed chi sao, cross armed
c) double handed chi sao

At each stage of training, one must progress from predetermined movements to random movements and then at the advanced stage, to training blindfolded.

It is important to understand the techniques used in chi sao may not apply to actual combat situations. However, the experience and the coordination achieved from these exercises are essential to combat.

Example of Contact Reflex

1) Ready position.

4) Opponent (right) punches.

2) Opponent (left) enters and contacts.

5) Opponent (left) interrupts movement.

3) Opponent (left) punches to the face.

6) Opponent (left) steps back with fut sao.

Example of Single-Handed Chi Sao

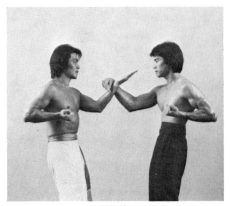

1) Opponent (left) uses tan sao against opponent's (right) fok sao.

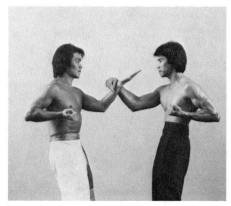

4) Return to original position.

2) Opponent (right) uses jut sao to deflect opponent's (left) palm strike.

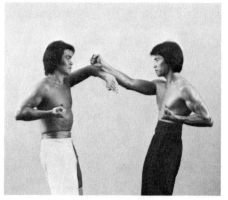

3) Opponent (right) uses bon sao to deflect opponent's (left) punch.

Chi Sao Exercise

Cross-armed chi sao is for training of contact reflexes at a front stance. This exercise is practiced in conjunction with single-armed chi sao and double-armed chi sao.

1) Opponent's right arms contact.

3) Opponent (left) palm strikes to the head and opponent (right) uses tan sao to deflect the attack.

2) Opponent (left) uses jut sao to create an opening for a right palm strike.

4) The opponents' right arms contact.

Continued

Chi Sao Exercise
Continued

5) Opponent (left) uses jut sao to create an opening for a right palm strike.

7) Uses jut sao to deflect the attack.

6) Opponent (left) palm strikes to the head and opponent (right) rotates his hand and ..

8) Opponent (right) then follows with a punch to the lower middle gate and opponent (left) uses kan sao to deflect the attack.

9) Opponent (right) then punches to the upper gate.

11) Opponents return to starting position with right arms crossed.

10) Opponent (left) uses tan sao to deflect the attack.

Example of Double-Handed Chi Sao Exercise

1) Opponent (left) uses bon sao and fok sao and opponent (right) uses fok sao and tan sao.

2) Maintaining fok sao, opponent (left) rotates bon sao to tan sao while oppoonent (right) rotates tan sao to bon sao.

3) Opponent (left) palm strikes and oppoonent (right) uses jut sao to deflect it. Return to number 1.

Example of Contact Reflexes with Blindfold

1) Opponent (left) is blindfolded and in ready position.

2) Opponent (right) comes in, grabs opponent's (left) leading arm and prepares to punch his head.

3) Through the point of contact, opponent (left) senses the direction of the oncoming punch and uses bon sao to deflect the punch.

D. Wooden Dummy

There are 108 combat techniques for the wooden dummy as well as 16 training techniques for kicks and leg blocks in the wooden cummy training sequence.

Wooden dummy training improves timing, speed of movement, power and accuracy of strikes, body mobility, arm and leg coordination, visual and contact reflexes, toughness of arms and legs, and flow of movement.

All combat techniques in Wing Chun come from those of the wooden dummy. It is vitally important to know the correct direction the body faces, how and when to apply the force while executing technique, and understanding the meaning behind each of the movements and their sequence.

Wooden dummy training also supplements sparring.

E. Bil Jee, Thrusting Fingers

This form trains finger striking with short bursts of arm movement, concentration of energy, and breathing.

When using the fingers for striking, the hand is prepared by tucking the thumb in and packing the fingers together so that they protect each other.

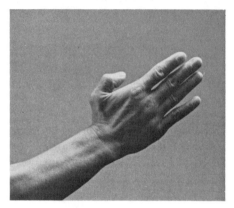

A prepared hand for finger thrusting.

In the advanced stage of bil jee, the fingers are allowed separation by compensating with wrist movements. When the fingers contact a target, the wrist must turn one way or the other to deflect the force of impact. The finger tips pivot into the point of contact. Without turning the wrist the finger joints are subject to severe damage from the force of impact.

Bil Jee Practice

1) Wing Chun guard.

2) Before contacting a target, keep fingers, wrist, and arm in a straight line.

3) The wrist turns up for vertical bil jee downwards. This action is similar to that of a fencing foil bending upon contacting a target.

Bil Jee Contacts a Target

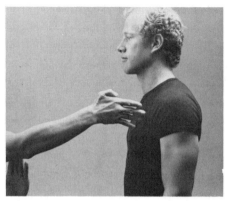

1) Downward vertical bil jee contacts a target.

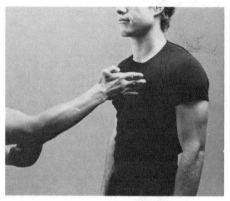

1) Upward vertical bil jee contacts a target.

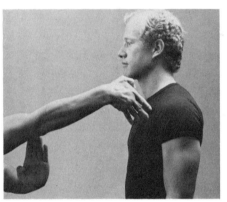

2) At point of contact, the wrist turns up and the finger tips pivot into the target.

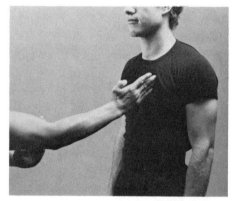

2) At the point of contact, the wrist turns down and the finger tips pivot into the target.

The same principle of turning the wrist applies to inward and outward horizontal bil jee. When striking inward, the wrist turns outward, and when striking outward, the wrist turns inward.

To perform bil jee successfully, training the wrist for cooperation and strength is essential to achieve striking movements that coordinate with the turning of the wrist. And there is no need to strengthen the fingers by hitting hard or semi-hard surfaces for bil jee. Fingers are strong from daily usage. Only concentration and the generation of power when striking are necessary to perform Bil Jee successfully.

Generally, a target can be any part on the upper torso and throat. There are numerous pressure points in those areas. Eyes can also be a target, but for a successful strike to the eyes, a practitioner must be fast and accurate.

Lastly, it is important to remember that bil jee can be deadly. Upon mastering this technique, practitioners are advised to use it only in emergencies.

Chapter 4

Wing Chun Fighting System

A. Central Line Theory

The *central line theory* defines the area a practitioner, without pivoting his hips, can cross his wrists at the lower, middle, and upper gates when in a neutral stance.

Demonstrations of Central Line Perimeter

Neutral stance. The wrists cross at the lower gate.

Neutral stance. The wrists cross at the upper gate.

Neutral stance. The wrists cross at the lower gate, right side.

Neutral stance. The wrists cross at the upper gate, right side.

Neutral stance. The wrists cross at the lower gate, left side.

Neutral stance. The wrists cross at the upper gate, left side.

Lower, Middle, Upper Gates:

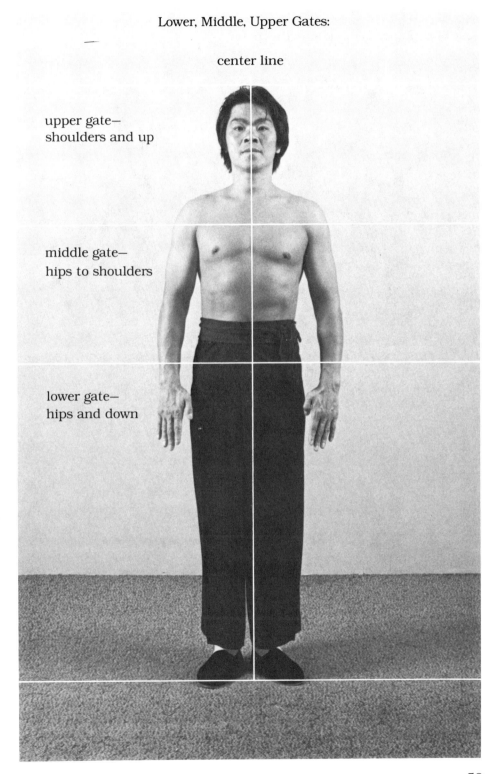

center line

upper gate—
shoulders and up

middle gate—
hips to shoulders

lower gate—
hips and down

The central line theory illustrates the limitations of the different stances. The following photos demonstrate this point.

1) Front stance. The wrists cross at the lower gate.

2) Front stance. The wrists cross at the upper gate.

The central line theory works effectively with a front stance.

1) Side-on position: The wrists are unable to cross low.

2) Side-on position: The wrists are unable to cross high.

From the side-on position, the lead arm can attack and defend, but the supporting arm can only defend.

Central Line Position, Wing Chun Guard

The central line position maximizes use of both arms for simultaneous attack and defense, and minimizes the practitioner's target area. With this position, the practitioner has the straight-line path available for attack, while an opponent has only the outside path, an increased distance.

Place both arms and elbows close to your central line. The leading arm is extended. The other hand is placed next to the leading arm's elbow.

Side view of Wing Chun guard, the central line position.

When using the central line theory, the practitioner must face the point of contact. The following photographs illustrate this point.

Incorrect Tan Sao

1) The practitioner facing directly front with tan sao in front of chest.

2) Incorrect tan sao cannot adequately stop a round punch.

Correct Tan Sao

1) Tan sao facing the point of contact. The body is turned slightly.

2) When facing the point of contact, tan sao easily deflects an opponent's arm and allows for simultaneous counter punch.

Incorrect Bil Sao

1) The practitioner executes bil sao directly in front of his body.

2) Incorrect bil sao cannot adequately stop a round punch.

Correct Bil Sao

1) With body turned slightly, the bil sao faces the point of contact.

2) When facing the point of contact, bil sao is much more effective.

B. Better Protection of the Body

With the elbows placed along the central line, you are protected at the middle gate when facing an opponent. In any attack to the lower gate, you need only to lower your arm along the central line to deflect or block the attack. Furthermore, by starting with the elbows and arms along the central line, you restrict the opponent's attack by forcing him to use the outer path, an increased distance.

A face off.

Wing Chun guard.

C. Independent Movement of Arms and Legs

A Wing Chun practitioner, preferably, chooses to use both arms and/or legs for attack and defense simultaneously. To achieve this versatility, each limb must have the ability, without restriction, to act independently from the other limbs.

The sil lum tao provides training for independent arm movement and chum kil and bil jee train the independent arm and leg movements.

Basically, Wing Chun uses arms for linear movements in attack, circular and linear movements in defense. The force is generated by coordinating the body movement with leg movement, and then is concentrated and generated from the elbow.

D. Ability to Interrupt Movements

In actual combat, one should not fully commit to a movement without reserving the opportunity to interrupt it. No matter how quickly the attacker can execute his technique, there is always a chance that the defender will be able to counter attack it.

If the attacker doesn't have the ability to interrupt his movement, either because of his momentum or because he is not prepared to interrupt, he will pay the price.

In Wing Chun training, the ability to interrupt movements is absolutely essential. The Wing Chun practitioner would prefer to sacrifice speed and power while executing a movement so that he will be able to interrupt it.

E. Wing Chun Punch

The Wing Chun punch takes a straight path and is driven by the elbow. With the elbow driving the punch along the central line, the body has better protection. This technique also enables easier recovery of defense after an attack.

Forming a Fist for a Wing Chun Punch

1) Left hand in open position.

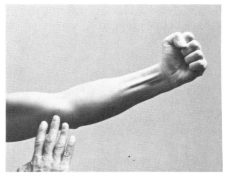

3) Fold thumb over fingers.

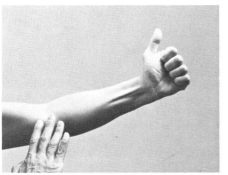

2) Lift thumb and fold fingers in tight.

Wing Chun Punch Demonstration	**Side View of Wing Chun Punch Demonstration**

1) Preparing for left punch.

1)

2) Left punch.

2) Side view of left punch. Note the right fist is under the left elbow to protect the body and the left fist remains vertical throughout the punch.

For a right punch, repeat on opposite side.

F. Five Stages of Combat

The first three stages of combat, the *before contact stage, contact stage*, and *exchange stage*, are determined by the relative distance between the two opponents. The fourth stage, *pursuit*, is applicable to any of the above stages. The fifth stage is *retreat*.

1) The Before Contact Stage

The *before contact stage* uses the neutral stance and Wing Chun guard on the central line. Without putting a foot forward, flexibility to move in any desired direction is increased.

Observe the defenders of a tennis, soccer, or basketball game. They, too, can't afford to commit themselves to a forward or backward stance which would hinder their mobility.

In one-on-one unarmed combat, without knowing who will attack and who will defend, it's an error to commit oneself to either by assuming the forward or side-on stance. These stances give a poor chance for defense on the blind side. The neutral stance, however, gives an all-around attack and defense opportunity.

At the before contact stage, use your eyes to focus on the nearest elbow and knee points. These points will key you to an intended move.

2) Contact Stage

The *contact stage* occurs when either or both fighters move in and reach a distance which enables contact with arms and legs, but not to main body targets.

At the contact stage, the central line is used at the outer perimeter with a front stance. The body is turned slightly so that the target is minimized. Information is coming in from the contact point as well as from visual

Before contact stage.

The contact stage.

observation. This enables the practitioner ample time to counter attack or initiate his own attack.

The contact reflex ability for close-range instant-response action and arm-leg maneuvering, gained through chi sao exercises, is tremendously useful at the contact stage.

3) Exchange Stage

At the *exchange stage*, contact to the main targets on the head and body is possible.

Other than low kicks, or spinning away with round or back kicks, generally, kicks are not favorable in the exchange stage.

Since Wing Chun puts defense first, at this stage the practitioner will put his guard a little higher than usual to protect his upper gate. His eyes constantly focus on the nearest elbow point because it will forecast the movement of that arm or fist.

When an arm, or both arms, have made contact with any part of an opponent's body, the practitioner should attempt to use the contact point as a guide to finding the opponent's nearest elbow point for controlling the opponent's balance and/or restricting the opponent's movement. With an opponent's elbow controlled, the practitioner can use it as a guide to finding the vital target on the opponent's head or body and maneuver to the blind side of the opponent, where he can deal with one arm at a time. Furthermore, the practitioner, aided by contact reflexes acquired from the chi sao exercises, is accustomed to using arms and legs at close range.

The ability to use both arms simultaneously for attack and defense is certainly an asset for the practitioner in the exchange stage.

4) Pursuit

When an opponent retreats, chase him. This stage is pursuit.

The general rule is that the practitioner must keep to the same side of contact to the opponent by covering his nearest elbow point and chase with

Exchange Stage

either half front step, front step, or full front step. Sometimes the contact is broken and then the practitioner is advised to re-enter to achieve further contact. Generally speaking, the front kick is very much favored in retreat. Extra care is warranted.

5) Retreat

Sometimes when one is in an unfavorable position, one must *retreat* in order to reorganize oneself.

A practitioner would generally use fut sao and backward step to get out of the situation. Often, a combination of fut sao and bil sao, together with a double backward step can be very useful. Nevertheless, after the retreat has been executed, one must return to the central line system for better protection.

Example of Wing Chun Retreat

1) Assume this starting position.

3) Turn and step back.

2) Bring front foot back to the rear foot.

4) Fut sao to cover defense.

The footwork for the retreat is very important. The practitioner must bring his foot back, close to the rear foot so that he can turn back and generally finish off the movement with the fut sao or bil sao.

Chapter 5

Bil Jee Form

A. The Beginning

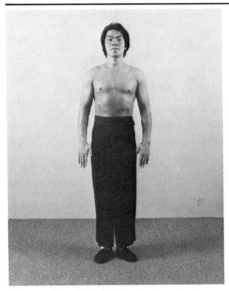

1) Stand with feet together, arms at sides.

2) Raise arms forward, palms down, to shoulder height.

5) Pull fists to sides, chest level, without touching the body.

6) Push hips forward and bend knees slightly.

3) Clench fists.

4) Turn fists outward and up.

7) Swing left leg forward and . . .

8) in a circular motion, outward to the side.

A. The Beginning

9) Pull right leg to the left leg and . . .

10) swing right leg forward and . . .

13) Raise forearms. Photo/captions 12 and 13 define central line area.

14) Clench fists.

11) in a circular motion, outward to the side. This is a neutral stance.

12) Cross forearms, left over right, palms down, at the mid-section away from the body.

15) Pull fists to sides, chest level, without touching the body. This is a neutral stance.

B. Bil Jee: Vertical Finger Thrusts and Horizontal Finger Thrusts

The pivoting directions of bil jee—upward, downward, inward, and outward—are optional in practice. However, when practicing this form they should be

1) Continuing from a neutral stance, bring left fist to center of chest away from body.

2) Left straight punch.

5) Cock left arm and prepare hand to strike.

6) Left vertical bil jee upward.

alternated with the same rhythm as demonstrated by master Cheung, who pivots with his own preference.

3) Cock left arm and prepare hand to strike.

4) Left vertical bil jee downward.

7) Cock left arm and vertical bil jee downward.

8) Cock left arm and vertical bil jee upward.

B. Bil Jee: Vertical Finger Thrusts and Horizontal Finger Thrusts

9) Turn left hand horizontally, palm down. Cock left arm and prepare hand to strike.

10) Left horizontal bil jee outward.

13) Cock left arm and left horizontal bil jee outward.

14) Cock left arm and horizontal bil jee inward.

11) Cock left arm and prepare hand to strike.

12) Left horizontal bil jee inward.

15) Turn left arm outward, palm up.

16) Left huen sao. Begin by bringing hand straight back. Rotate it inward and . . .

B. Bil Jee: Vertical Finger Thrusts and Horizontal Finger Thrusts

17) downward and . . .

18) outward and upward and . . .

21) Pull fist to side, chest level, without touching the body. This is a neutral stance.

Reversing all directions of right and left, repeat entire section B from #1 before continuing to next section.

19) turn palm inward vertically and cock it back at the wrist.

20) Clench fists.

C. Elbow Strike and Horizontal Bil Jee from Below Striking Arm

1) Continuing from a neutral stance, step to a right side neutral stance, move right elbow center and . . .

2) step to left side neutral stance. Raise left elbow and . . .

5) right elbow strike.

6) Drop elbow and begin stepping left to a . . .

3) left elbow strike.

4) Drop elbow and begin stepping right to a right side neutral stance. Raise right elbow and . . .

7) left side neutral stance. Raise left elbow and . . .

8) left elbow strike.

C. Elbow Strike and Horizontal Bil Jee from Below Striking Arm

9) Prepare for right horizontal bil jee from below left arm.

10) Right horizontal bil jee inward.

13) Simultaneously step back toward a neutral stance and . . .

14) swing left arm across to left side. Fut sao.

11) Begin stepping forward to a front stance and prepare left horizontal bil jee from below right arm.

12) Left horizontal bil jee inward.

15) Raise left arm and . . .

16) bring left arm down to center of chest semi-extended along central line with right guard hand next to left elbow.

C. Elbow Strike and Horizontal Bil Jee from Below Striking Arm

17) Simultaneously right horizontal bil jee inward from below left arm, and pull clenched left fist to side, chest level, away from body.

18) Turn arm outward, palm up.

21) outward and upward and . . .

22) turn palm inward vertically and cock it back at wrist.

19) Right huen sao. Begin by bringing hand straight back. Rotate the palm inward and . .

20) downward and . . .

23) Clench fist.

24) Pull right fist to side, chest level, without touching the body. This is a neutral stance.

Reversing all directions of right and left, repeat entire section C from #1 before continuing to next section.

D. Elbow Strike and Horizontal Bil Jee from Above Striking Arm

1) Continuing from a neutral stance, step to a right side neutral stance, move right elbow center, and . . .

2) step to a left side neutral stance. Raise left elbow and . . .

5) begin stepping forward to a . . .

6) left front stance. Right horizontal bil jee inward and simultaneously place left hand above right arm.

3) left elbow strike.

4) Prepare right bil jee from below left arm and . . .

7) Left horizontal bil jee inward while withdrawing right arm from below.

8) Simultaneously step back toward a neutral stance and . . .

D. Elbow Strike and Horizontal Bil Jee from Above Striking Arm

9) swing left arm across to the left side. Fut sao.

10) Raise left arm and . . .

13) Turn right arm outward, palm up.

14) Right huen sao. Begin by bringing hand straight back, bending at wrist. Rotate palm inward and . . .

11) bring left arm down to center of chest semi-extended along the central line with right guard hand next to left elbow.

12) Clench left fist and pull to side, chest level, and simultaneously right horizontal bil jee from below left arm.

15) downward and . . .

16) outward and upward and . . .

D. Elbow Strike and Horizontal Bil Jee from Above Striking Arm

17) turn palm inward vertically and cock it back at wrist.

18) Clench fists.

19) Pull left fist to side, chest level, without touching the body. This is a neutral stance.

Reversing all directions of right and left, repeat entire section D from #1 before continuing to next section.

E. Elbow Strike and Vertical Bil Jee from Below Striking Arm

1) Continuing from neutral stance, step to a right side neutral stance, move right elbow center, and ...

2) step to a left side neutral stance. Raise left elbow and ...

3) left elbow strike.

4) Prepare right bil jee from below striking left arm.

E. Elbow Strike and Vertical Bil Jee from Below Striking Arm

5) Bring left foot next to right and . . .

6) right horizontal bil jee.

9) Simultaneously begin stepping back toward a neutral stance and . . .

10) swing left arm across to left side. Fut sao.

7) Step to front stance and . . .

8) left vertical bil jee downward.

11) Raise left arm and . . .

12) bring left arm down to center of chest semi-extended along the central line with right guard hand next to left elbow.

E. Elbow Strike and Vertical Bil Jee from Below Striking Arm

13) Clench left fist and pull to side, chest level, and simultaneously right vertical bil jee.

14) Turn right arm outward, palm up.

17) continue rotation outward and upward and . . .

18) turn palm inward vertically and cock it at the wrist.

15) Right huen sao. Bring hand straight back. Rotate palm inward and . . .

16) downward and . . .

19) Clench fists.

20) Pull fist to the side, chest level, without touching the body. This is a neutral stance.

Reversing all directions of right and left, repeat entire section E from #1 before continuing to next section.

F. Elbow Strike and Vertical Bil Jee from Above Striking Arm

1) Continuing from a neutral stance, step to a right side neutral stance, move right elbow center, and . . .

2) step to left side neutral stance. Raise left elbow and . . .

5) bring left foot next to right and . . .

6) right horizontal bil jee from below striking left arm.

3) left elbow strike.

4) Prepare right horizontal bil jee from below striking left arm and . . .

7) Simultaneously step forward to a front stance, withdraw right arm slightly, move left hand to right elbow and . . .

8) left vertical bil jee from above right arm.

F. Elbow Strike and Vertical Bil Jee from Above Striking Arm

9) Simultaneously begin stepping back toward a neutral stance and . . .

10) swing left arm across to left side. Fut sao.

13) Clench left fist, pull it to side chest level, and simultaneously right vertical bil jee.

14) Turn right arm outward, palm up.

11) Raise left arm and . . .

12) bring left arm down to center of chest semi-extended along central line with guard hand supporting left elbow.

15) Right huen sao. Bring hand straight back. Rotate palm inward and . . .

16) downward and . . .

F. Elbow Strike and Vertical Bil Jee from Above Striking Arm

17) continue rotation outward and upward and . . .

18) turn palm inward vertically and cock it at the wrist.

19) Clench fists.

20) Pull right fist to side, chest level. This is a neutral stance.

Reversing all directions of right and left, repeat entire section F from #1 before continuing to next section.

G. Kan Sao

1) Continuing from neutral stance, raise left arm with elbow bent, hand at head level. The right arm crosses the chest with hand supporting left arm and . . .

2) step to left side neutral stance. Retaining both elbows at central line to protect upper and middle gates, the left forearm with palm up rises slightly, and the right arm with palm down extends diagonally down. This is left kan sao.

3) Raise right arm with elbow bent, hand at head level. The left arm crosses the chest with hand supporting right arm and . . .

4) step to right side neutral stance. Retaining both elbows at central line to protect upper and middle gates, the right forearm with palm up rises slightly and the left arm with palm down extends diagonally down. This is right kan sao.

G. Kan Sao

5) Step to left kan sao.

6) chamber left leg for front kick and . . .

9) Low left side kick.

10) Step forward diagonally to a . .

7) left front kick.

8) Rechamber leg and lean back to begin low left side kick. Bon sao by positioning left elbow with forearm across body to protect from underneath and right guard hand near left elbow for support.

11) left front stance and left huen sao. Right hand supports left elbow.

12) Simultaneously step to a left side neutral stance and raise left forearm, bringing it a-long central line.

G. Kan Sao

13) Left jut sao. Right hand supports left elbow.

14) Left huen sao from left side neutral stance while turning to right side neutral stance.

17) Step to a left side neutral stance and left jut sao.

18) Step to a right side neutral stance and . . .

15) Left huen sao at right side neutral stance.

16) Raise left forearm and bring it in along central line. Jut sao.

19) left huen sao and . . .

20) step forward and . . .

G. Kan Sao

21) left pak sao with reverse palm strike.

22) Preparing for fut sao, right arm pulls back, right foot steps back and . . .

25) bring right arm down to center of chest semi-extended along central line with left guard hand next to elbow.

26) Lower right arm and turn left arm inward, palm up, and raise it slightly.

23) right arm swings to side. Fut sao.

24) Raise right arm and . . .

27) Reverse palm strike with left arm while pulling right fist to side, chest level.

28) Lift palm and arm slightly.

G. Kan Sao

29) Left huen sao. Bring palm back, rotate palm inward and . . .

30) downward and . . .

33) Clench fists.

34) Pull left fist to side, chest level, without touching body. This is a neutral stance.

Reversing all directions of right and left, repeat entire section G from #1 before continuing to next section.

31) continue rotation outward and upward.

32) turn palm inward vertically, and cock it at the wrist.

H. Quan Sao

1) Continuing from neutral stance, the right arm crosses mid-section with hand close to left elbow, and left forearm extends frontward with palm up and . . .

2) step to a left side neutral stance and begin pushing right forearm out with palm inward, diagonally up along central line. Simultaneously raise and turn out left elbow and forearm, palm downward, along central line and . . .

5) step to right side neutral stance and begin pushing left forearm out with palm inward diagonally up along central line. Simultaneously raise and turn out right elbow and forearm, palm downward, along central line and . . .

6) left tan sao with left elbow along central line with forearm and palm upward, and right bil sao with right elbow shoulder level, forearm facing out, extending diagonally across body. This position is right quan sao.

3) right tan sao with right elbow along central line with forearm and palm upward, and left bon sao with left elbow shoulder level, forearm facing out extending diagonally across body. This position is left quan sao.

4) Left arm crosses mid-section with hand close to right elbow, and right forearm extends frontward, palm up and . . .

7) Step to left quan sao, left side neutral stance.

8) Left heel kick to right side.

H. Quan Sao

9) Low left bon sao and chamber for low left side kick.

10) Low left side kick.

13) Right leg steps forward and . . .

14) strike with both palms. Po pi tserng.

11) Step forward left diagonally.

12) Preparing for po pi tserng, turn left elbow and forearm out and down. Then both arms extend slightly with wrists together, right over left, palms outward.

15) Turn palms up and . . .

16) double huen sao. Bring palms back and rotate them inward and . . .

H. Quan Sao

17) downward and . . .

18) outward and upward.

21) Bring right foot in and . . .

22) step back and across right and . . .

19) Clench fists.

20) Pull fists to sides, chest level.

23) plant right foot and . . .

24) bring left leg to right and . . .

H. Quan Sao

25) swing left leg forward and . . .

26) in a circular motion, outward to the side. This is a neutral stance.

Reversing all directions of right and left, repeat entire section H from #1 before continuing to next section.

I. Fut Sao and Bil Sao

1) Continuing from a neutral stance, step to left side neutral stance and bring right forearm across lower gate. Left palm supports right elbow.

2) Bring right foot next to the left foot.

3) Step forward sideways and swing right arm from below to the side. The left palm supports right elbow, palm faces out.

4) Turn body right, slightly. Place left hand under right arm.

119

WING CHUN BIL JEE

I. Fut Sao and Bil Sao

5) Simultaneously bring left foot next to right foot and withdraw right arm along central line keeping left hand below right arm.

6) Left horizontal bil sao from below right arm.

9) Right horizontal bil sao from below left arm.

10) Prepare and repeat left horizontal bil sao from below right arm.

7) Withdraw left palm along central line and keep right arm below left elbow and . . .

8) continue withdrawing left palm and prepare for left bil sao.

11) Withdraw left palm and . . .

12) left palm strike to the right. Right hand supports left elbow.

WING CHUN BIL JEE

I. Fut Sao and Bil Sao

13) Slightly turn torso frontward and withdraw left palm to right shoulder. Left hand supports right elbow.

14) Turn body frontward, left foot steps back and . . .

17) bring left arm down to center of chest semi-extended along central line with right guard hand supporting left elbow.

18) Bring right foot next to the left. Move right palm over left.

15) out to a neutral stance simultaneously swinging left arm across to left side.

16) Raise left arm and . . .

19) Swing right foot forward and back toward a neutral stance and prepare for right bil sao.

20) Right bil sao.

WING CHUN BIL JEE

I. Fut Sao and Bil Sao

21) Pull left fist to side and right bil sao.

22) Turn right palm up.

25) outward and upward and . . .

26) turn palm inward vertically and cock back at wrist.

23) Right huen sao. Bring palm straight back and rotate it inwards and . . .

24) downward and . . .

27) Clench fist.

28) Pull fist to side, chest level. This is a neutral stance.

Reversing all directions of right and left, repeat entire section I from #1 before continuing to next section.

J. Double Arm Grab and Vertical Bil Jee

1) Continuing from a neutral stance, bring palms out in front and away from chest.

2) Push arms out.

5) Right pak sao with left arm supporting right elbow.

6) Left vertical bil jee downward.

3) Grab with both hands.

4) Step to a right side neutral stance.

7) Withdraw left arm, turn, and face front.

8) Swing left arm up diagonally to the side and . . .

J. Double Arm Grab and Vertical Bil Jee

9) bring the left arm down to center of chest semi-extended along the central line with right guard hand supporting left elbow.

10) Clench fist.

13) huen sao. Bring palm straight back and rotate it inward and . . .

14) downward and . . .

11) Pull left fist to side, chest level, and right vertical bil jee.

12) Turn right arm outward, palm up and . . .

15) outward and upward and . . .

16) turn palm inward vertically and cock it back at the wrist.

J. Double Arm Grab and Vertical Bil Jee

17) Clench fist.

18) Pull fist to side, chest level. This is a neutral stance.

Reversing all directions of right and left, repeat entire section J from #1 before continuing to next section.

K. Torso Bend

1) Continuing from neutral stance, raise elbows, open hands, and bend forward slightly.

2) Simultaneously thrust both arms downward and bend torso forward.

3) As the body begins to rise, swing both arms higher than torso.

4) Torso rises with arms extended in line with torso.

K. Torso Bend

5) Swing both arms, palms out, out to sides.

6) Wing Chun guard.

9) Right punch and withdraw left arm.

10) Left punch and withdraw right arm.

7) Close right fist and prepare to punch.

8) Left punch and withdraw right arm.

11) Bring right fist out with left.

12) Turn arms outward, palms up.

K. Torso Bend

13) Double huen sao. Bring palms straight back and rotate them inward and . . .

14) downward and . . .

17) Clench fists.

18) Pull fists to sides, chest level.

15) outward and upward and . . .

16) turn them inward vertically and cock them back at the wrist.

19) Bring left foot next to right.

20) Place arms at sides and stand upright.

Chapter 6

Techniques

Entry Technique

1) Right bil sao to occupy central line of upper gate.

3) Bringing right knee up to cover the middle gate, begin moving in.

2) To occupy the lower gate, move right knee across to the left.

4) Step in.

Side View of Entry Technique

1)

3)

2)

4)

Entry Technique to the Outside of Opponent's Leading Arm

1) Ready position.

3) . . . steps outside opponent's (black) front leg to cover his leading elbow with white's left arm.

2) Opponent (white) enters with bil sao, bringing his left knee across and up to protect the middle gate and . . .

4) White uses bil jee to the throat.

Entry Technique to the Inside of Opponent's Leading Arm

1) Ready position.

3) steps outside opponent's (black) leading foot and covers the elbow and leading arm from the inside.

2) Opponent (white) enters with bil sao, bringing his left knee across and up to protect middle gate and . . .

4) White applies pressure to Black's elbow and uses bil jee to his throat.

Entry Technique Against Front Kick

1) Ready position.

3) White uses left foot to stop front kick and simultaneously covers Black's leading elbow point with left arm.

2) Opponent (white) enters with bil sao, bringing left knee across and up to protect middle gate. Opponent (black) prepares front kick.

4) White steps in and controls Black's elbow and uses bil jee to his throat.

Entry Technique Against Round Cross from Open Side

1) Ready position.

3) Opponent (black) begins left cross from open side.

2) Opponent (white) enters with bil sao, bringing his left knee across and up to protect middle gate.

4) White covers the left cross at elbow point, and simultaneously steps in with bil jee to the throat.

Bil Sao Technique. A Counter Against Round Punch.

1) Ready position.

2) Simultaneously right side step by placing left foot behind right foot and bil sao.

3) Step forward with right foot and larp sao with right arm.

Fut Sao and Bil Sao Against Double Round Punch

1) Ready position.

4) Black swings right round punch.

2) Opponent (black) begins a left round punch.

5) White uses bil sao to stop punch and . . .

3) Opponent (white) covers punch with fut sao.

6) bil jee to throat.

Elbow Technique and Finger Thrust

1) Ready position.

4) left elbow strikes Black's temple and . . .

2) Opponent (black) steps in with reverse punch.

5) follows with bil jee to the eyes and . . .

3) Opponent (white) deflects punch using larp sao and . . .

6) bil jee to the mid-section.

Larp Sao Technique

1) Ready position.

4) bring Black's arm to the side and . . .

2) Opponent (black) steps in with right straight punch.

5) prepares to strike with . . .

3) Opponent (white) uses double larp sao to . . .

6) bil jee to the ribs.

Huen Sao Technique Against Round Punch

1) Opponent (white) in ready position. Opponent (black) begins round punch.

3) White stops round punch by using kan sao and . . .

2) Black steps in with round punch and white begins kan sao.

4) front kicks Black's ribs and . . .

5) rechambers leg for another strike and . . .

7) uses right huen sao, bringing Black's right arm to the side and . . .

6) lower side kicks Black's knee and . . .

8) uses bil jee to Black's ribs.

Quan Sao Technique

1) Ready position.

4) traps Black's arm.

2) Opponent (black) begins straight punch.

5) White then sweep kicks Black's knee and . . .

3) Opponent (white) begins quan sao and . . .

6) rechambers and . . .

7) kicks Black's groin.

8) Rotating his arms, White brings Black's arms to the side and . . .

9) moves in for a double palm strike.

Counter Against Round Kick

1) Ready position.

3) Black round kicks. White stops the kick at the knee with kan sao, then . . .

2) Opponent (black) chambers for round kick. Anticipating a round kick, opponent (white) side steps and begins kan sao.

4) places left hand on top of Black's knee and pushes it down as he uses bil jee to the ribs.

Counter Against Back Kick

1) Ready position.

4) pushes the leg at the knee to the side.

2) Preparing for back kick, opponent (black) spins around.

5) White then covers Black's elbow and . . .

3) Opponent (white) uses tan sao to deflect the back kick and . . .

6) uses bil jee to the neck.

Counter Against Straight Punch

1) Ready position.

2) Opponent (black) steps in with straight punch and opponent (white) deflects it with pak sao.

3) White steps in and uses bil jee to mid-section.

Counter Against Round Punch

1) Ready position.

4) White kicks Black's mid-section and . . .

2) Opponent (black) steps in with left round punch. Opponent (white) stops punch with tsun sao and . . .

5) steps forward and . . .

3) larp sao to Black's left arm while side stepping to prepare for kick.

6) bil jee to throat.

Counter Against Double Punches

1) Ready position.

3) Black withdraws right arm and prepares for right round punch.

2) Opponent (black) steps in with straight right punch.

4) Black attempts right round punch and White turns and faces his elbow point and simultaneously uses larp sao to stop the punch at elbow point and horizontal bil jee to the liver.

Counter Against Double Round Punch

1) Ready position.

4) White brings his left arm around Black's right arm and slides his right arm along his left arm in order to turn it around.

2) Opponent (black) steps in with left round punch and opponent (white) uses pak sao to stop the punch from inside of his arm.

5) White moves to blind side of Black.

3) Black right round punches and White turns and uses right pak sao to stop punch.

6) White then steps in and uses horizontal bil jee to the ribs.

157

Against Quar Tsui (Big Swinging Punch)

1) Opponent (white) in ready position. Opponent (black) begins big swinging punch.

3) White pushes Black's right arm away and steps into his blind side.

2) Black steps in with big punch and White stops it with kan sao.

4) White then uses reverse vertical bil jee to Black's ribs.

Against Front Kick and Round Punch

1) Ready position.

3) Black steps forward and round punches. White covers the round punches at Black's elbow.

2) Opponent (black) steps in and front kicks. Opponent (white) steps and deflects the kick with gum sao.

4) White uses bil jee to the ribs.

Conclusion

Wing Chun Bil Jee, The Deadly Art of Thrusting Fingers is written as a reference for the intelligent martial artist. Master William Cheung is particularly qualified to meet this task. Internationally recognized for his expertise and accomplishments in Wing Chun, he brings over 30 years experience, research, and devotion to this endeavor.

Wing Chun is a scientific approach to fighting. Though the Bil Jee form is central to this book, the Wing Chun system, central line theory, and techniques demonstrated are offered by Master Cheung with hopes of illustrating that a scientific approach to the martial arts is beneficial to both the arts and practitioners.

Presently, Master Cheung's headquarters is the Australian Kung Fu Academy, 26A Corrs Lane, Victoria, Australia 3000.